A Light Amidst
Illuminating Menta

WRITTEN BY
Gina Capobianco

ARTWORK BY
Shannon Feldmann

FOREWARD BY
Sheri Fink

Books by Gina Capobianco

Cognizant Introspection
Conscious Connection
Curative Quest: Mental Health, Hope, and Healing

A Light Amidst the Darkness:
Illuminating Mental Illness and Suffering
By Gina Capobianco

Text copyright © 2020 by Gina Capobianco

ISBN: 978-0-578-77592-0
FIRST EDITION

Praise for A Light Amidst the Darkness:
Illuminating Mental Illness and Suffering

"Writing can give us a mirror into important life experiences such as depression. In *A Light Amidst the Darkness: Illuminating Mental Illness and Suffering*, author Gina Capobianco uses the power of poetry to show us the struggles of one caught in both the throes of serious depression and anxiety. In reading her words you can experience how completely debilitating depression can be as it weighs one down with pain, darkness, and an inability to act. Capobianco's words deftly explore the challenges a patient of mental illness faces with the health care system. She takes readers from the hurt of a careless misdiagnosis to the office of a kind physician who guides her gently into relaxation and the courage to move forward. Capobianco writes, "My pen is an instrument of healing." Indeed, it is." ...Sandra Marinella, author of *The Story You Need to Tell—Writing to Heal from Trauma, Illness, or Loss.*

"This is a very powerful collection of poems that doesn't flinch when describing the impact of depression. But crucially it also gives hope, which is what each of us needs with this illness. I really loved it."...James Withey, Author of *How to Tell Depression to Piss Off* & Editor of *The Recovery Letters*

"Gina Capobianco should be commended for her visceral storytelling through her poetry. Her poems are deeply personal, at times unrelenting in their honesty, and always captivating to the ear. I give her latest offering my highest praise."...Edward Portillo, Mental Health Advocate

"Gina provides valuable insight for people struggling with a mental illness who want to live a normal life!"...David Dicken, Crisis Counselor & Creator of MakeSomeoneGreatToday.com

DEDICATIO

To all who are suffering silen
mental illness. May you one d
feel safe enough to share your st

TABLE OF CONTENTS

Acknowledgments

My life has been blessed with many lights, people without whom my healing would not be possible. They have lit my path and been by my side in their own ways. They have made A Light Amidst the Darkness: Illuminating Mental Illness and Suffering possible.

Thank you to Shannon Feldmann, Carol Nichols, and Sarah Usmani. You are the greatest friends anyone could ask for. Thank you for being by my side and always being there with your love and support. I treasure our friendship.

Thank you to Dr. Richard Klein, PhD. You have guided me for many years and been a light amidst the darkness.

Thank you to Dr. Catherine Sullivan, MD. I am grateful that you have helped me find the light of healing with your support and genuine care. Thank you for providing the chance for me to be heard.

Thank you to Pam Martin and to Carol Harrison (may she rest in peace). You have guided and supported me for almost 30 years. I would not be who I am without you.

Thank you to Shannon Feldmann for the amazing artwork on the cover of A Light Amidst the Darkness: Illuminating Mental Illness and Suffering.

Thank you to my family.

Thank you to Sheri Fink for always encouraging me and for being an inspiration.

Thank you to these medical professionals who make the effort to understand and are true examples of what is right in health care:
Dr. Maria Kronen, MD, Greta Vines, PA–C, and Cristina Rosales, PA–C.

Thank you to Zsuzsi Steiner of Zsuzsi Photography.

Thank you to Michelle Morgan for editing and AJ Cosmo for the cover and page layout.

Foreword

Gina Capobianco is an authentic force for good in the world. Her work as a writer, teacher, speaker, and advocate for mental health care inspires me. In *A Light Amidst the Darkness: Illuminating Mental Illness,* she continues her legacy of transforming lives.

I first met Gina at a book-signing event in 2015. Her humble demeanor hid the talented artist bubbling inside. I could tell that we were kindred spirits. Since then, we've become friends and I've had the privilege of mentoring Gina to help bring her recent books into the world to make a bigger impact.

Over the years I've known her, I've watched Gina grow to stand in her power and blossom to become more courageous and confident in speaking her truth. In doing so, she gives others the inspiration and permission to speak theirs. Her valiant mission is to remove the societal stigma that forces people who suffer from mental illness and mental health disorders to remain silent.

Gina and I share the perspective that mental health is an important part of our overall well-being. She has overcome personal adversity in her life to serve as a beacon of light for others. This brave, heart-centered woman faces depression and anxiety on a daily basis and shares her experiences to demonstrate that there's always hope. It's easy to see why she was named one of the "World's Best Speakers on Mental Resilience," an honor she shares with the Dalai Lama and Eckhart Tolle.

Using her unique experiences, poetry, teachings, and motivational speaking, she helps bring light and hope to those who suffer while cultivating empathy and understanding in those who have not personally experienced these challenges.

As someone who makes a living writing books and giving talks that inspire and empower people to embrace their authenticity and take action toward their dreams, I fully support Gina's mission. Everyone can benefit from her message. It's needed now more than ever before.

No matter how dark our world (internally or externally) may seem at times, Gina reminds us there is always a light amidst the darkness.

- Sheri Fink
Inspirational Speaker, Best-selling Author, and Founder of *Whimsical World*
www.SheriFink.com
@Sheri_Fink on Instagram & Twitter
@SheriFinkFan on Facebook

PREFACE

My intent in writing *A Light Amidst the Darkness: Illuminating Mental Illness and Suffering* is to give meaning to the mental health struggles I have experienced throughout my life and to provide a sense of bonding to others who suffer. If even one person is able to relate to my story, then it has all been worth it.

Throughout this preface I will use the terms *mental health disorder* and *mental illness* interchangeably. While my experiences have been with depression and anxiety, I believe the same coping strategies can be applied to other mental health disorders.

For years I attempted to hide my depression and anxiety. Since there were no outward manifestations it was relatively easy to mask my mental illness, but I was ashamed of having a mental illness. It was something I felt I could not talk about openly with anyone other than my psychologist. I did not think anyone else would understand. I believed that depression and anxiety were my lot in life, and I had to just silently deal with them alone.

That is what stigma does. It forces those who suffer to remain silent. It forces us to hide in our darkness. Merriam-Webster defines *stigma* as "a mark of shame or discredit; a stain." The stigma surrounding mental illness leaves people feeling ashamed; feeling as if they are marked. This stigma is often subtle, although at times it can be overt.

When a person who is struggling with depression is told by a well-meaning friend to "just smile" or to "focus on the positive," that is stigma at work. The friend does not understand that it is not that simple. Depression is an illness. It is not a choice. One cannot just smile and be happy. Stigma also rears its head when doctors or other medical professionals assume that a patient's physical symptoms are "just anxiety" because that person has a mental health diagnosis. I will devote a section to health care later in this preface.

Stigma makes it difficult to discuss mental health with family and friends. I did not want my family to know about my mental health issues. I feared they would not understand. At times I feared their rejection. However, it is the lack of understanding that is the most difficult to deal with when opening up about a mental illness. Too many people do not understand.

In my darkest days I wanted to be alone. Isolating myself seemed like the best option. It protected me from others and protected others from me. At times I wanted to hurt myself. I had this recurring thought that physical pain was more bearable than mental pain. Of course, that is not true, but it is often what I believed.

DEPRESSION AND ANXIETY

Depression began to invade my life when I was 14 years old. It is difficult to describe those early days. I remember feeling numb; not being happy; not wanting to live. They were feelings I did not understand. The world seemed dark. To a teenager it was a scary place. Those feelings kept intensifying, but I did not know how to explain them. I did not know I could ask for help. No one reached out. So, I kept everything inside.

I was diagnosed with depression when I was 20 years old. The doctor prescribed medication and I started going to therapy. During this time, anxiety also made its presence known. I can clearly remember my first episode of anxiety. My chest tightened. I felt shaky. Everything was closing in on me. I remember needing to get away. I had to find an open space. Those feelings have been taunting me for a long time now.

Living with depression and anxiety is not easy. In fact, some days it feels impossible. I have been asked what it feels like. I am not sure there is one specific answer. People experience depression and anxiety in different ways. Of course, there are some commonalities. For me there is a darkness that is all-consuming when I am depressed. I feel weighted down. At times I cannot motivate myself to do even the simplest of tasks. I feel numb and in pain at the same time. The depression tears at my hope, leaving me feeling empty. Often when the depression takes over, I just want to lie down in the dark and hide.

When the anxiety takes over, I feel like *I* have no control. My chest hurts. At times I have been convinced that I was having a heart attack because the pain was so intense. I feel shaky. Sometimes the shaking is visible. Other times it is inside of me. I feel like I am struggling to breathe even though my breathing is normal. My thoughts become rushed. I cannot stop thinking. These thoughts gain control over me.

Sometimes when the depression and/or anxiety are strong, I can still put up a façade and function. Other times I need to be alone. Over the years I have learned many coping skills. Of course, medication and therapy are important, but equally important are the coping skills I employ.

There are a handful of coping skills that I rely on when the depression and anxiety are bad. One of those is writing poetry. I discovered writing as a teenager and have not stopped since. See the *Writing to Heal* section for more on this.

I also walk. Going for walks is often very calming for me. I have read that exercise is important when dealing with a mental illness. My psychologist tells me this all the time. Walking is my exercise of choice. It is especially helpful when I pair it with another one of my coping skills, which is listening to music. For me it is rock music that is most calming. It may sound strange that rock music is calming for me, but there is just something about guitar riffs and a bass drum that soothes me.

Sometimes I listen to meditations. If my anxiety is keeping me awake at night, I often listen to a meditation and attempt to control my breathing. Related to this is self-hypnosis, a relaxation tool that helps me calm my thoughts and relax my body at the same time.

Having a support system is also important for coping with mental illness. I have three close friends who are my support system. They are people I can be open with about my struggles. They listen when I need someone to listen. Sometimes just being there is enough. Other times they remind me to use my coping skills. They encourage and support me. I would not be where I am today without their support.

Depression is a lonely illness. It is important to have supportive friends and family. Sure, I have a psychologist and a psychiatrist whom I can turn to, but sometimes I need a friend to be with me. Being open about my mental health has allowed my friends to understand me. This enables us to have a stronger relationship and prevents my mental illness from interfering with our friendship.

WRITING TO HEAL

When I am depressed, I feel alone. It is hard to believe that others will understand. I tell myself that no one else knows what it is like. It feels awful. Depression can be a very lonely illness. Yet in the midst of the loneliness, I often feel the need to be more alone. It is a difficult aspect of depression to explain. I do not think I can explain it in simple conversation.

Perhaps that is why I have always been drawn to writing poetry. I have been writing poems since the earliest days of my depression over thirty years ago. In my writing I am free to express all that I usually keep locked up inside of me. I can write in verse all that the stigma tells me I cannot say aloud. Poetry is a healing instrument for me. It has been my lifeline, my family, and my friend. As I write, I pour out my thoughts and feelings. I say what I need to say. The pages of my journals always listen. These pages become my sounding board. They are the safety net that prevents me from plummeting into total darkness.

When I am writing poetry, I can be me. I can describe what depression and anxiety do to me. My words express how depression squeezes the life out of me; how it steals my hope. Through poetry I can explain anxiety. My words can paint a picture of the physical symptoms of anxiety. They can transcribe the words that are jumbled in my mind during a period of anxiety.

The beauty of poetry is the way it expresses the ugliness of mental illness. Poetry brings to life the darkness I feel and allows it to escape from within me. That release provides the light of healing. It gives me an opportunity to understand what I am going through in life. Poetry provides me with perspective. It is that perspective that allows me to open up to others and to heal.

I started writing poetry as a teenager, maybe 14 or 15 years old. There is a lot that I do not remember about that time period. The one thing I do remember is that there was something wrong. Looking back on it, I know that is when the depression began. I remember being in pain. It was not a physical pain, but it consumed me just the same. There was a numbness inside of me. At times I did not want to live. I felt isolated, but I did not know how to ask for help. In fact, I am not even sure I knew I needed help.

This is where the poetry came into play. I am not sure how I started writing or what made me pick up a pen the first time. Writing poetry became a part of me. I was always writing. My first journal was a small, red spiral notebook. In time I would have several of those notebooks. I carried them with me everywhere. Those journals were full of the poems I wrote. I am not sure how good that early poetry was, but I do know that I wrote about how I felt. I wrote about the pain; the numbness; the hopelessness. At the time, I did not realize my writing was my lifeline.

Today, after more than thirty years, I am still writing poetry. I have written countless lines. The words have poured out of me at times. Other times the words have barely trickled from my pen. The healing power is still present. Every time I write a poem, a bit of light emanates from within me.

For thirty years the power of writing has led me on a journey. It has been by my side at the deepest depths of my depression and anxiety. It has followed me into the light of healing. My poetry shares my message of hope. Even the darkest poems offer a piece of me that someone, somewhere, can relate to in their own way.

Writing is a form of communication. Perhaps therein lies the purpose of my writing. It allows me to communicate the feelings and thoughts I carry within me. I communicate with myself when I write. The words become committed to the page. What I do with the words then becomes my choice.

In recent years I have chosen to share the poetry I write. I choose to communicate with others. My hope is that there is something in my poetry to which others can relate. In relating, I hope these words can bring the light of healing to others who suffer from mental illness and a sense of understanding to those who have not experienced mental illness. If these two things occur, my writing has served ia purpose beyond the catharsis it offers me.

Writing poetry, as I have mentioned, is my lifeline. It provides me with healing and hope. Writing allows the poison that mental illness creates to flow out of me.

I cannot underestimate the power writing has provided in my healing journey. Poetry is my preferred genre of writing. I have employed journaling at times. At other times free writing loosens my ability to write. I truly believe there is a story within each of us that wants to be told. I tell my story through poetry. For many of us telling that story through writing is therapeutic. I do not have the educational degrees in this area to defend it. However, experience is a great teacher. Experience is something I have plenty of in this area. I know what rolling my pen across the pages of a journal has done for me. Typing words on a keyboard strengthens me. As I see my words transform into lines, see those lines become poems, I experience a powerful healing.

Lab Coat Diaries

One area where I think an unintentional stigma against mental health exists is in health care, itself. Some of my own experiences have brought this stigma to light. I believe medical professionals would benefit from more training with regard to mental health issues. They must understand that mental health is a part of overall health.

Being in a doctor's office has never been easy for me. My anxiety kicks in even if I am comfortable with the provider. My experiences in medical environments have been mixed. The more difficult visits have led to my needing to write and resulted in poems. As with other difficult times in my life, I have turned to poetry to help me cope.

Perhaps the hardest part of medical visits for me is feeling misunderstood by doctors and physicians' assistants (PAs). Often, I feel like they see my mental health diagnosis and assume that is the problem. They slap labels on me that they do not truly understand. The poem "Misdiagnosed" is my expression of what it felt like when I saw that a PA had put the wrong diagnosis in my chart. I wrote a poem to say the things I could not get myself to say aloud. I realize that I should have spoken up to the PA. The poem was the first step. Now I have to advocate for myself.

Let me explain what lies behind my hesitancy to advocate for myself. A few years ago, I had an awful experience with a primary care PA. She was very insensitive about my mental health, and her words wounded me deeply. She probably did not even give a second thought to what she said, but it destroyed my trust in health care providers. Her words felt like a dagger being thrust into me. Maybe she did not truly understand the power of her words, or did not care, but as a person who has a mental illness, I felt the sting of them.

It took me two weeks to gather the courage to speak up. Even though I tried to stand up for myself, I am still haunted by her words three years later. I never saw this PA again. She never apologized or even acknowledged the lasting pain she had caused.

This is the price of the mental health stigma.

Some good came of this incident. It made me aware that the stigma against people with mental health disorders exists in health care, and it encouraged me to become an advocate for mental health care. My intent is not to generalize or slam health care providers. However, there are individuals like this PA, whose ignorance affects patients. I still have a difficult time trusting medical providers. Even though I know my current provider is different, I still become anxious. I still am hesitant to trust. That is not fair to me or to my current provider. I wrote a poem to help me flesh out these feelings and the thoughts I still have. The poem is entitled, "Insensitive Words Remain with Me," and can be found in the Lab Coat Diaries section.

Primary care providers can be the frontline defense in the battle against mental health disorders. Too often we think of doctors as only tending to physical health, but they need to look at total health. That means addressing a patient's mental health, too. Mental health issues are often camouflaged as physical symptoms. A primary care provider can be the first to recognize this and refer the patient to an appropriate mental health care provider.

It was a primary care provider who made a dramatic difference in my life. I was at a very difficult point. My depression and anxiety were manifesting as physical symptoms. I was having chest pain. I could not sleep. I was barely getting through life. I was on more prescriptions than I could even count. My psychiatrist at the time would add new medication and increase dosages of other prescriptions every time I saw her. Then one day, I had an appointment with my primary care provider, a physician's assistant. She asked me a question that would become pivotal in my healing.

"Why are taking that medication that way?"

She was referring to a medication I had been taking too often. I did not know how to answer the question. I merely said, "Because it is what my psychiatrist told me to do." I will never forget the look in her eyes.

She said, "But that's not how you are supposed to take that medication."

We talked about all of the medications I was prescribed. I could not even tell her why I was taking each one. She had me come in again the following week. We went through everything I was taking. I was hit with the reality that I was addicted to one of them. With the help of this PA I was able to stop taking the medication I was addicted to and reduced the number of other medications I was taking. She helped me realize that the psychiatrist was just masking my mental health issues with prescription medication.

Once I was off some of the medications I felt as if a fog had been lifted. I found a new psychiatrist. It took trying a few before I found the right one. I was able to free myself of the addiction to a medication that was hurting me. None of this would have happened if a primary care provider had not taken the time to take an interest in my care and really listen to what I was saying. This PA did more than just monitor my physical health. She changed my life.

This is the role a primary care provider can and should provide. They need to see the patient as a whole person. It is important that the provider not only listen to what the patient is saying, but also what the patient is not saying. Oftentimes it is the physical symptoms that a patient is having that hold a clue to his or her mental health.

I am a strong believer that we need to break down the stigma against individuals with mental health disorders that exists in health care. There needs to be more training for health care professionals about mental health. They need to learn from mental health care providers. They need to listen to the stories of those of us who live with mental health disorders. We need to build an understanding that mental health is a part of overall health. This will not be an easy task, but I believe it is one that can be accomplished. I implore doctors, PAs, nurse practitioners, and nurses to open their hearts and listen to their patients. Be aware of mental health. Make an effort to understand what your patients live with daily. Find it in yourself to empathize. So many people struggle with mental illness. One day you might find yourself in the darkness of depression or the battle with anxiety. Be the provider you would want for yourself.

GRIEF

Grief is a pain we all go through at some point in our lives. Writing can assist us in dealing with the pain of losing a loved one. It can allow us to process our thoughts and say the things we can no longer tell our loved ones.

When someone dies, an obituary is usually written. This provides a glimpse into the person's life story. Obituaries, while written in times of sadness, are usually filled with cherished memories. In a similar way, a eulogy is often given at a funeral or celebration of life. Here we find more stories of the person's life. We remember our loved ones through stories; through the memories we share. We share the happy moments, the struggles, the day-to-day encounters. This sharing is a human need. It is a part of the healing process. For me it is where writing fits into the process. I have poetry to remember my loved ones. Some of it I have shared. Some of it I have kept to myself.

As of this writing, I have been lucky that I have not lost many people in my life. Five deaths have had an impact on me. Three of those people, my grandparents, Burl and Kay Gray and Stella Capobianco, lived long lives. So, while their losses were painful, they were easier to accept than the other two. I wrote poems about my grandparents to help me remember the good times with them. By committing those memories to paper, I will always have them when I need comfort.

My father, Daniel Capobianco, passed away at the young age of 64 from cancer. The disease took him too fast. It took a while for me to write my feelings about his death. My father did not want a funeral. This was hard for me to accept. How do you honor a life without the final goodbye given at a funeral? How do you share the stories of that person's life? Since there was no funeral, I was left holding the stories in my heart. Eventually, the emotions captured by those stories flowed out of me in the poem "Cancer Ripped You Away." I looked at all my father was no longer experiencing; at what cancer took from him and his family. I wrote about it. I also wrote a couple other poems for my father, which are included in the section, Grief.

Another difficult loss for me was the death of my coach/mentor/friend, Carol Harrison. Cancer tore her away too soon and I had a hard time accepting her death. Writing about her helped. I was able to share my feelings and let the pain escape. There is something special about being able to write my emotions into poems. I had the opportunity to read one of those poems at her celebration of life. As I read the poem, I saw the expressions on the faces of others who had gathered to celebrate her beautiful life. There was a sense of relating. We were all grieving and the words many us of shared connected us and provided a salve for our wounds. That is the power of writing and telling stories. I have written six poems about Carol. It was definitely a difficult loss for me and one that I needed to cope with through writing.

A Few More Thoughts

A Light Amidst the Darkness: Illuminating Mental Illness and Suffering, along with my other books (*Cognizant Introspection, Con-*

scious Connection, and *Curative Quest: Mental: Mental Health, Hope, and Healing*), is my attempt to share my experiences as an individual with a mental health disorder. It is my attempt to open more dialogue about mental health and break down the stigma through awareness. If we, as a society, are going to reduce the stigma surrounding mental health, we must engage in meaningful conversations. We must openly discuss how mental illness affects people. My poetry has allowed me to start many conversations about mental health. I found connection with others who struggle with the effects of mental illness. Just as importantly, my poetry has brought awareness to people who have not experienced depression and/or anxiety.

These are honest expressions of how depression and anxiety have impacted my life. Many of the poems are dark. Despite their darkness, I believe it is important to include them in this book. These poems represent the effects of mental illness. These poems are my reality. Even in moments of healing, I know the darkness is lurking not too far away. It can creep in at any moment. I have learned that darkness is a part of me. Expressing the thoughts fueled by mental illness allows me to heal. It is amidst the darkness that we find the light of healing.

A DARKENED PATH

DEPRESSION WON

Depression is a vise.
Its grip is soul crushing.
For so long it has held me in its claws;
Reduced me to a shadow of what I could have been.
Depression haunts me,
Mocks me.
I have become a punching bag.
Taking blow after blow.
Battered and bruised by depression, I fall to the ground.
I attempt to rise, but stumble.
My desire to heal withers.
Tears sting my eyes.
A sense of resignation envelops me.
I fought, but in the end the depression won.

DARKNESS REEMERGES

I struggle to understand what is happening.
Everything was going so well,
But now I am tumbling.
My life is a mess again.
I cannot sleep.
Simple acts take up most of my energy.
I am surrounded by a fog.
My focus is obscured.
I do not want to do anything.
I have no motivation,
Lack the desire to be a part of anything.
Spinning, my world is spinning.
Darkness rushes in once again.
I have so much to be happy about,
But I cannot enjoy it.
What is wrong with me?
Why can I not just snap out of it?
My mood drags me down.
Lack of sleep paralyzes me.
I do not want to succumb to the darkness,
But fear I will.
I have fought for so long.
The light shined briefly.
I felt so much better,
But then the darkness reemerged;
Delivered its crushing blow.
I have fallen again.
I wonder if I can ever get up.
I do not understand the waves of depression.
Will they ever remain just a ripple?
Will I ever be strong enough to surf these waves?
I thought I was doing so well.
Now I am faced with the reality that the darkness will never fade.
Darkness is always lurking;
Always haunting me.
I cannot escape the depression that grips my life.

Unknown Memories

I cry for the self I have lost;
The once-happy child I do not remember.
Was there ever such a child?
I do not remember childlike happiness.
No memories of carefree days.
Childhood is a blur,
Darkened to the point of being unrecognizable.
I try to remember, but nothing reaches my consciousness.
My only memories are of the darkness.
The depression gripped me, locked me within in its grasp.
That is where my memories begin.
As if my life started in adolescence with the first chilling gust of
depression.

Shades of darkness fill my mind.
Blacks and grays create the color scheme of my memories.
Light is snuffed out whenever it emerges.
I hide within the shades of gray.
Afraid the memories will wake up and
Confront me.
Force me to face a reality I do not remember.
I fear the unknown memories.
Their grip upon my life tightens.
Despite the fear, I cannot go on this way.
Is there something I need to know in the memories I have forgotten?
Or will I emerge more damaged than I already feel
My cries continue as the child I once was is lost forever.

THE SMOTHERING HAND
OF DEPRESSION

The smothering hand of depression suffocates me.
I gasp for breath as I search for meaning in my life.
The depression bears down upon me,
Crushing my desires and dreams.
Underneath the weight of depression, I am weak.
I hide from life.
Afraid to push back against the depression that has been a part of my life for so long.
I do not remember life without it.
As I struggle, my hope dwindles.
The hand presses down more firmly.
I cannot get back up.
The smothering hand of depression has taken my life.

A Gnawing Sense

A gnawing sense of not wanting to be a part of anything.
A deep-seated desire to withdraw from life.
I am plagued by these feelings.
They emanate from deep within me.
As I long to escape from my life, I cry over all that I am missing.
Two sides of a double-edged sword pass through me.
I feel pain, sharp and piercing;
My flesh torn.
Still my heart beats.
I hear the echo of my cries.
Haunting me; mocking me.
Life seeps out of me.
I see my essence draining.
That gnawing sense has become my reality.

A DECISION

Confusion settles in.
A decision looms,
But I am at a loss.
A choice I am not prepared to make weighs heavy upon me.
I seek out advice;
Ask the opinions of those I trust.
They offer me their thoughts; try to guide me.
Yet the decision remains mine to make.
So many times, I have hidden from decisions;
Allowed fate to take charge.
I cannot hide this time.
There is too much at stake.
A decision must be made and
I must make the choice.

PATHS

Sometimes I think I have found the right path.
My journey has been long and arduous, but I have kept walking;
Continued when there was no light in sight.
Many times I have stumbled,
Found myself battered and bruised, yet still I keep trudging.
Many of these "right" paths have led me in the wrong direction;
Left me in darkness.
So, my search continues, and I journey on.
Afraid of the darkness, yet
More afraid of not finding the light.

BLIND

Staring into the mirror I look right through the image staring back at me.
I do not notice my own reflection.
Something deeper calls to me,
But I do not recognize it.
Staring into the mirror I see nothingness.
A blank face gazes back at me as if questioning,
"Do you not see my pain?"
I feel the familiar ache within me, but fail to make the connection.
The ache and the pain are one.
As I stare into the mirror, I am blind to my own essence.

FACES

Familiar faces penetrate my soul
Leaving a jagged scar.
Memories I cannot comprehend torment me.
Sleepless nights and angst-filled days.
Emptiness gnaws on my soul.
I fight back the tears, unaware of the source of my pain.
Hazy glimpses of the past cloud my vision.
The past is so unclear.
I wonder what brought me to this point.
Shaped by incidents I no longer recollect,
I shake with an unknown fear.
The faces haunt me,
Ridicule me for not remembering.
Unable to make sense of the faces,
I scream in silence.

HAUNTED

I am haunted by a past I do not remember.
Tension and fear serve as reminders,
But they do not tell the story.
I contemplate opening the window to the past.
Consider letting in the unknown.
It is an agonizing proposition.
The thought of knowing the truth scares me.
I have moved so far beyond my past.
Yet it feels as if it is right beside me.
The past has found a place to nestle inside of me.
It is comfortable there even though I am not.
Going back would open the wound;
Cause more harm than the understanding it might bring.
So, I leave the window closed.
Keep the past shut out and
Attempt to live in the present.

LOOKING BACK

In the empty hours of the day
And sleepless hours of the night,
I pass the time alone.
Wondering why I have no companionship;
Questioning my life choices.
I look back in time and see the nothingness,
The quiet days, the lackluster events of my life.
In each one, I am alone;
A solitary figure with tears in my eyes.
So many times, I have tried to reach out
But each attempt leads to false hope.
Now, as I sit in my solitary confinement, reflecting,
I realize my life has passed me by.
I must accept what my life has become;
Recognize the blame lies within me.
My hope has been tarnished.
Left me alone.
As my life continues in solitude.

AMBITION

Abundant ambition has left me scarred.
So many attempts to better myself have ended in disappointment.
I was once filled with hope.
Now I am empty, drained of desire.
An unfilled canister sitting in the dark.
I approach life differently now.
Timid;
Unwilling to take chances;
Afraid to live.
Ambition has destroyed me.

ANOTHER DAY

It is a day like any other.
I awake before the sun,
Still tired from a restless night.
My day begins,
Monotonous in every aspect.
I hide behind my façade;
Try to fake a smile
But inside my mind thoughts are racing.
Continuing through the day, I pretend that I am okay.
Somehow, I get through another day.
Night falls.
My façade disintegrates.
I try to make sense of all the whirling thoughts
But I am defeated.
I have let my guard down.
Allowed the darkness to win once again.

AGAIN

Every year it happens.
I should be better prepared for it.
By now I know what to expect and
Know how it will make me feel.
That does not make it any easier.
The pain will still surface.
The feelings of worthlessness will overtake me.
I will long for an escape but remain trapped.
My feelings do not matter just as I do not matter.
My wants are not even acknowledged.
I go through the motions;
Push down the depression building inside of me.
It festers, but I cannot let it show.
All of this just to pretend the holidays still hold meaning
When in my heart I know they do not.

CHRISTMAS EVE

Once there was laughter and smiles.
Many voices carried conversations;
Smiles on the faces of the young and old;
Trays overflowing with traditional food.
We ate and talked, laughed and shared.
Soon a knock would draw our attention to the door.
Much to the children's delight, Santa would appear.
The old ones smiled; the young ones filled with eager joy.
After Santa returned to his busy sleigh ride, gifts were exchanged.
More laughter and smiles;
A Christmas filled with family.

This year there is no laughter;
No smiles between generations.
Memory longs for those family times
But they have been lost for years.
Some have found new traditions.
Others trapped in the loneliness of remaining memories.
Christmas Eves of the past have disappeared,
Never to be replaced.
A dying memory, a last link to happier family times.
Christmas Eve, forever lost.

THE DAWN OF A NEW YEAR

The dawn of a new year;
A chance to begin anew.
Each year I find myself clinging to this same hope,
Only to find myself in tears.
The new year brings opportunities
But it also carries more of the same pain.
The shadows follow the ringing of the new year;
A cloud of darkness always lurking.
Sunshine attempts to break the hold darkness has on me.
I tell myself this is the year I will hold onto the light.
Depression's hold on me allows the shadows to take over;
Gives them power.
A new year clouded in darkness just as it begins.
A new year, no different than the years before.

SOCIAL ANXIETY

A casual social situation freezes me.
Thoughts paralyze my mind
And I cannot interact.
A coolness passes through me.
I do not know what to say,
So I sit quietly.
Passively, I watch the interactions around me.
I wonder where my confidence has fled;
Question why this happens so often.
People chat, engage in laughter as they converse.
I try to keep up with the banter
As I shrink smaller and smaller.
But it is no use.
I cannot fit in with others.
So I learn to make up excuses;
Reasons to stay away.
I feel foolish and
At times my tears fall.
Socially fearful,
I am destined to be alone.

UGLY HEADS

Just when I start to believe I have overcome my struggles
The depression and anxiety rear their ugly heads once again,
Sending me spiraling down without a safe place to land.
The darkness floods my vision.
Tears fill my eyes.
I attempt to refocus on the positives, but it is no use.
I lack the strength to continue the fight.
Hope has been sucked out of me.
The light has been extinguished.
All of my effort has been wasted.
My freefall into the depths of darkness continues.
I have lost control.

TEARS BEHIND THE FACADE

I have created a façade to face each day;
Prevent others from seeing my trepidation.
My fear resides deep within me,
Hidden beneath layers of scars,
Where no one can laugh at me.
I am alone with my fear.
Uncontrollable feelings bubble to the surface.
The fear consumes me, causes me to tremble.
But I stand firm,
Do not allow myself to weaken.
Fear has mocked me, belittled my emotions.
Yet still I stay hidden.
My tears flow at times,
Hot and salty, reminding me that I am alone.
Wounded, but proud, I hide my tears;
Remain in the shadow of my façade.

NIGHTTIME

Anxiety consumes my nighttime thoughts,
Racing through my body, leaving me on edge.
I cannot get the thoughts to stop.
Incessant chatter keeps me awake.
I tell the thoughts to stop, but they do not listen.
The words continue pestering me, reminding me of my fears.
The anxiety is real.
It never leaves me, but at night it reaches its peak strength.
I am awake most of the night, fighting with the thoughts,
Leaving me exhausted and weak the next day.
The anxiety wins the battle
But I have shown up for the war,
Ready for the next battle despite my fatigue.

SLEEP ELUDES ME

Awake once again.
The middle of the night has become my companion.
We spend so much time together.
I long to sleep, but my eyes remain open.
The thoughts in my head continue to whirl.
My body will not relax.
The middle of the night seems to welcome my alert presence.
The stars outside my window mock me.
Darkness laughs.
I call out to sleep; wonder where he hides.
I close my eyes; try to fool myself into believing I am asleep.
The joke is on me.
Sleep eludes me night after night.
Awake once again.

Trapped in the Grip of Insomnia

Insomnia fuels my writing.
The words flow when I cannot sleep.
I write before I know what I want to say.
There are so many words trapped inside of me begging to be released.
I do not know what they are trying to say.
I only know they must be written, must be heard.
Allowing the words to take over, I escape the tossing and turning of insomnia.
I am wide awake now.
The words take over.
The words are in charge now.
Sleep will not visit me tonight.
The insomnia has won, given power to the words.
I can only write;
Let the words leave my fingertips and fill the page.
I spend too many nights like this.
Trapped in the grip of insomnia.
Unable to relax and welcome the regenerating power of sleep,
I continue to write,
Hoping some bit of insight will surface.
Perhaps then this insomniac writing will have a purpose.

MY SLEEPLESS DANCE

Sleepless night number _____.
I have lost track.
As usual, despite the darkness of the hour, I am awake.
My eyes will not close.
My brain keeps running with meaningless thoughts.
I have exhausted many sleep remedies.
Medications do not work.
Breathing exercises have little effect.
Meditations do not still my mind.
The sweet scent of lavender mocks me.
Music distracts me, but I do not fall asleep.
Night after night I engage in this dance.
One step forward, two steps backward.
My eyes grow heavy yet sleep eludes me.
Soon daylight will seep through the curtains.
Reminding me that the night has slipped away once more.
I will face another day without rest;
Somehow manage to drag myself through it.
Only to be awake again at night.

SLEEP MOCKS ME

I do not know what to do anymore.
Every night is the same.
I cannot sleep.
I am wide awake.
I have tried everything, but to no avail.
It is two o'clock in the morning.
I should be asleep like most normal people.
The sleeping pill I took had no effect on me.
It used to get me a few hours' of sleep,
But the pill no longer works.
Reading, music, herbal tea,
Lavender spray and lotion,
Meditation and hypnosis.
I have tried them all.
Nothing works.
I feel the need to sleep, but once I turn out the light,
Sleep mocks me.
The heaviness of my eyes tells me I need sleep
But I just stare.
Night after night the problem grows worse.
I do not know what to do.
I have given up trying.
All I can do is occupy the time and
Wait for the sun to rise.

SEEKING COMFORT

Tears stream down my face.
My vision blurs.
I am alone yet again.
The emptiness consumes me,
Leaving a gaping hole inside of me.
I shiver as the warm tears sting my eyes.
My heart becomes numb.
My body crumples into bed.
Pulling blankets over me, I attempt to comfort myself,
But I am too aware of how alone I am.
Aware of the penetrating silence surrounding me,
I continue to cry.
Heaving sobs replace the gentle sighs.
Curled up under the blankets, I hide;
Seek comfort,
But there is no comfort to be found.

ISOLATION

An isolated being
Fragile and afraid
Hides behind four walls,
Rarely letting others inside,
Pushing away attempts to reach in.

The isolation becomes comforting,
A welcomed warmth in an icy realm;
Her safety net in an unsafe world.
Others cannot harm her as she is
Slipping deeper into isolation.

An isolated being
Secure behind self-erected walls
Huddles in a corner where
No one can see her
As she gives up on life.

DREAMS

Dreams are lies.
Dreams hold no power.
Dreams crush unsuspecting souls.
Dreams are jokes.
Dreams lead us to believe in fairy tales.
Dreams promise happily ever after.
Dreams lose their power when reality sets in.
Dreams become wild and farfetched.
Dreams become unattainable.
Dreams are lies.

THE WORDS

I sat and read a book,
Riddled by anxiety; drowning in depression.
Craving distraction, I focused on the words on the page;
Sought understanding and comfort in the words of another.
But the words inside of me begged to be released.
I tried to force them down,
Tried not to listen to their piercing message.
The words inside of me kept resurfacing until I finally set the book
down.
I turned on music to drown out the words;
Begged the guitar riffs to take me away.
Still I could find no relief.
The words grew louder and louder, echoing in my head.
I turned the light out hoping to snuff out the words' power.
But their power intensified.
Curled up in a ball, I covered my ears;
Tried to block the words.
Still I could find no relief.
My mind is overloaded, maxed out,
No longer able to comprehend its own messages.
My mind struggles to make sense of life's simplest operations.
I am consumed by the messages of anxiety and depression.
No longer hopeful of relief, I have become complacent.
Accepting the power of these words, I fall to the ground in despair.

THE SHUTTERS OF MY DREAMS

The shutters of my dreams have been pulled taut.
No light seeps in.
Darkness, pitch-black darkness.
Without light I have no hope.
My dreams melt to the floor like a Salvador Dali painting.
Dreams that once seemed so bright lose shape,
Lose hope.
The darkness has snuffed out my dreams.

LIES

Within my mind lies are hurled.
I am the primary target.
Voices tell me I am incapable;
Tell me I cannot be successful.
The words weigh me down,
Crush my confidence.
The words become my reality despite their root in lies.
I can no longer tell the difference between words of support and
cruel lies.
The words just spin within my mind.
I am paralyzed, unable to move forward,
Afraid to take simple chances.
I am left shattered, too weak to make any effort.
My heart once held hope.
My mind believed in me at one time.
Now the voices with their destructive words have won.

THE BROKEN WINGS OF A DREAM

The broken wings of a dream prevent me from soaring,
Keep me grounded in the reality of my depression.
I once had hope,
Believed in something greater than my present.
Now I search through empty landscapes,
Alone and dejected.
My wings clipped.
My hope shattered.
I no longer dream.
Emptiness consumes me,
Drags me through the dirt.
The broken wings of a dream have left me to languish in despair.

MY LIFE

A life wasted.
Days spent staring at the walls.
My life has never had a purpose.
I am just taking up space.
So much of my time is spent alone.
I cry, but no one sees my tears.
I have done nothing with my life.
It has all been just a waste.
There is no meaning in my life;
No reason to continue.
I have wasted my life.
Never really lived.
The walls close in on me.
Still I keep staring,
Afraid to make the changes I need to make.
I am fully aware that I am at fault.
I am alone because I am not worth anyone's time.
It is me who does not belong.
Life was wasted on my existence.

FOREVER ALONE

It was foolish for me to expect a different outcome.
Nothing is ever going to change.
My life is what it is.
I am alone.
I always will be.
How could I have thought life would change?
It has been this way for so long.
Nothing will ever change.
This is how I was meant to live.
Sometimes I wonder if life is even worth living.
I am not sure there is a point.
Loneliness is so painful.
It is a controlling bitch,
Ruining any chance at happiness that may have once existed.
Life will never change.
I am forever alone.

LIFE ELUDES ME

I tell myself that I can get through this,
Somehow summon the strength to allow being alone to be enough.
It becomes more difficult with each passing day.
Living like this takes a toll on me.
I have no more hope.
Joy eludes me.
I am trapped in a life that I can no longer live.
I have tried to be happy,
Attempted to insert myself into life.
But I do not fit.
I never really have.
It is time I stop trying.
Some things are just not meant to be.

SHADOWS IN THE DISTANCE

Do I have anything left to draw upon?
It seems I have lost everything.
I tell myself it is just the depression talking;
Try to believe it.
Despite my efforts I just cannot believe there is anything for me.
My loneliness isolates me.
It becomes more difficult to interact.
I feel myself pulling away.
The smile I tried to hide behind has vanished.
The positive thoughts I told myself have been overrun by the negative voices.
Everything seems hopeless.
I look around me and see nothingness.
In the distance there are shadows, but they move farther away.
I am alone.
A familiar darkness settles upon me.
The depression has won.

MY JOURNEY

My journey stops and starts,
At times following the light;
At other times, plunging into the darkness.
The hills and valleys I travel upon match my moods.
My pace slows as the journey becomes too much.
I am barely moving forward,
Making so little progress.

In the good times light guides me and I smile,
But the darkness is always lurking,
Pushing the sun behind the clouds.
My smile fades.
The downward trek begins again.
I seem to go down a little farther each time
It becomes more difficult to climb up.
The light becomes dimmer.

My journey is not yet over,
But I am not sure I can hang on much longer.

VOICES

How do I learn not to listen to the voices in my mind?
The voices are so loud.
Overpowering.
Shouting all that is wrong with me.
Telling me what I cannot do.
I tell myself not to listen;
To ignore the words,
But their volume intensifies.
I have grown tired of these thoughts.
They tear me down.
Ridicule me and
Make me feel worthless.
I have heard these words for so long.
They are my constant companion.
The chatter in my mind has become overbearing;
The only messages I hear.
I have fought the words,
Told myself not to listen,
But I am weak.
The words hold a power over me.
Please, someone tell me how I can stop listening to these voices.
Tell me how to silence them.
Then perhaps I can find peace and
Become more than I am now.
Without the negative chatter I might find I have a lot to offer;
That I am able to do more than I thought.

BURSTS OF LIGHT

THE PHANTOM

A phantom wraps its arms around me.
It is cold against my skin.
The phantom came to me long ago and has never left.
It haunts me during the night,
Wreaks havoc in the light of day.
Holding secrets, keeping me from understanding, and
Preventing me from truly living.
The phantom knows the source of my pain,
Mocks my attempts to decipher the pain's origin.
The phantom has power over me.
Uses it to maintain my brokenness.
I attempt to seek answers, but the phantom is always hovering
over me.
At night I lie awake wondering how to make the phantom
disappear,
But worry the phantom has the answers I have been searching
for.
It is all too much for me.
Within my mind, I am screaming.
What does the phantom want from me?
Does it want me to understand something?
Or is it keeping a secret from me?
I cannot continue in this way.
I have reached my breaking point.
The phantom knows, which only gives it more power.
The cold presence of the phantom tightens its arms around

me.
I feel a chill move through me.
"What do you want from me?" I scream at the phantom.
Its grip loosens.
"Come with me," cackles the phantom,
But I root myself firmly to the ground, afraid.
The phantom stares into my eyes.
"You must see the past to understand the pains;
Open your eyes to a time you have repressed."
I do not know if I can trust the phantom,
But my desire to heal emerges.
Somehow I know I must follow the phantom.
It reaches out a grayish hand.
I reach for it and let it take hold.
As I follow the phantom, there is pitch darkness.
Scenes of my life flash by in reverse.
We are moving back in time, further and further.
I am afraid.
I do not want to relive these moments,
But the phantom continues.
Darkness swirls around us.
I feel past pains reemerge.
Shutter against the phantom's embrace.
Memories circle us.
I catch glimpses, but do not understand.
Questioning if I really want to know the root of my past pain,
I pull against the phantom.
The phantom's cackling voice urges me to continue.
My strength is waning.
I do not have the will to continue,

But the phantom pulls me.
As we walk, memories become more nebulous.
I cannot make sense of what I am seeing,
But I feel the pain as it reemerges.
Suddenly I know the memories are better left hidden.
With every bit of strength I possess, I pull away from the phantom;
Turn and flee back to the present,
Leaving the phantom and painful memories behind.

THE LIGHT

Light penetrates the darkness.
Seeing clearly for the first time in ages,
I question my whereabouts;
Wonder how I have reached this place.
There is no one else around.
I begin to notice how truly alone I have allowed myself to become.
The glowing light allows me to see all that I have been missing.
I realize I have erected makeshift walls around myself.
Kept out those who would have helped along with my fears.
The light clarifies my reality.
My eyes are truly open for the first time.
In the darkness I was able to isolate myself.
Keeping my fears at bay prevented me from understanding them.
Now with the light I see the work I must begin in order to save my-
self.
Allowing the light into my life is the key.
Hope travels with the light.
Friends ride in on waves of light.
I open my eyes and allow the light to take control.

A TINY RAY OF LIGHT

Depression replaces the joy I had been feeling.
Brought down again by a darkness I can never truly escape.
Depression haunts me, always hiding nearby.
It throws its shroud upon me when I least expect it.
As if laughing at me for daring to believe life could be worthwhile.
Depression does not want me to experience the light of healing.
I get so close.
I can feel the warmth.
I begin to smile.
Foolish, so foolish!
Depression wraps itself around me;
Extinguishes the light.
I am ready to give in, but I see a faint ray of light.
Slowly I move my attention to this tiny ray.
I feel it; gain strength from its glow.
The depression may have me now,
But I know the light is still with me.
Healing is within my reach.

MY CRACKS

Picking up the pieces, I attempt to reassemble my life.
Like shards of glass the pieces fit together leaving visible cracks.
On the surface the cracks represent brokenness,
But upon further inspection the cracks demonstrate healing;
The mending of wounds.
I am a cracked vessel,
Complete in my brokenness.
I honor my cracks,
Recognize their strength.
Without these cracks I would not be the person I am today.
The cracks are scars, reminders of the wounds I have overcome;
Symbols of my strength.

AN INVISIBLE ILLNESS

I see it in the eyes of others.
They wonder how I can have an illness
When I seem to function so well.
My illness is invisible at times,
But it is always there.
Plaguing my mind;
Hindering my life.
I hold so much of the pain inside;
Pretend the physical symptoms are not real.
Mental illness is often silent on the outside.
Others do not understand what I go through each day.
They assume I am okay.
Sometimes I even tell them I am.
It is my attempt to normalize how I really feel,
But it is a lie.
Mental illness hurts.
Invisible at first glance;
Devasting when truly seen.
If others could see the torment,
Maybe they would understand and
Life might be a little easier for me.
The pain of an invisible illness is hard to explain.
So, I do my best to hide it,
When really I should explain it to anyone who will listen.
Let others know what it is like;
Raise awareness and
Allow myself a chance to heal.

ANXIETY'S CONTROL OVER ME

Anxiety, why do you fight me?
Night after night we battle.
Your words ring incessantly in my mind.
Sending jitteriness pulsating throughout my body.
I try to push your thoughts out of my head,
But they remain, beating like a drum.

Anxiety, your power over me tears me down;
Leaves my consciousness battered and bruised.
Your words are deafening.
I try to fight back against your torment,
But my strength withers.

Anxiety, when will you let me go?
Remove the chokehold you use to contain me.
Your strength is more than I can bear.
My mind and body are trapped,
Held ransom by your mounting control over me.

Anxiety, I feel myself giving into your nagging chatter;
Unable to control the pains you create within my body,
I lose hope.
Anxiety, you have the control.
You could set me free,
But instead you mock me.

Anxiety, you have won the battle,
But I will continue to fight this war.

AMBITION

Some days I wonder where my ambition has escaped.
I spend my time in a daze,
Not really sure what I want to do.
I go through the motions of life,
A mere shadow of the person I am meant to be.
Most days I am alone.
Being alone enables me to avoid life's pleasures,
But it brings me down,
Buries me in depression.
It is difficult to find ambition when darkness surrounds me.
So, I just pass the time; watch the clock.
With each passing moment I become more detached.
I do not like what my life has become,
But struggle to find another way to live.
My lack of ambition leaves me crumbling,
On the verge of giving up.
Still I must face each day,
Somehow fight through the apathy, and find the ambition to continue.

JOY

There is joy in life.
We can find it if we take the time to search for it.
Joy is hiding,
Waiting for us to discover its presence,
Uncover its gifts.
Joy is a mystery
Revealed when the moment is right.

LIGHTS

I will try to be positive.
Attempt to focus on the lights in my life.
It is so difficult
But I know I must try.
I am struggling;
Losing my hold on life.
I cannot let go.
There are lights.
I know they are there within my reach.
If only I could stretch out my arm,
Grab hold and cling to one.
I will focus on just one light at a time;
Be positive for a moment.
Maybe if I can focus for just one moment,
I will find there are more lights within my reach.
Grasping, I may find enough light to brighten my life.
Be positive.
I say the words over and over again.
Allow myself to hear the words.
Positive thoughts will lead to the lights.

THE LEDGE

The ledge beckons me,
Urges me to make a decision;
Choose between where I am and where I am headed.
Visions of yesterday cloud my mind.
My thoughts ram into each other,
Making little sense.
I look out over the ledge,
Wonder how my life has reached this moment.
Once I had dreams, plans for the future,
But now I have spent so much time alone.
Never fulfilled those dreams,
Never attempted those plans.
Now a decision looms.
I have walked out onto this ledge alone,
Determined not to turn back;
Ready to move forward,
Yet unsure of myself.
The ledge appears to be an end,
But it is not.
There is another ledge above it,
Barely within my reach.
I question if I can take the step.
It is my only hope.
The only chance I have left to take.
It is not the first ledge that beckons me;
Rather the higher ledge calls out,
Reassures me with its stone construction.
With closed eyes I gather my strength and
Reach within myself one more time.
Shakily I step off one ledge up onto the higher ledge.
Filled with trepidation I pull my other foot to this new height.
A sigh emerges from me.
Relief fills me.
Hope shines upon me as I begin life anew.

A FRIEND

A friend sits next to me.
It comforts me to know she is there.
Words do not have to be exchanged.
Presence is powerful.
Just knowing she is there eases my anxiety;
Enables me to relax.
So much is going on around us.
The outer world is in turmoil,
But for a brief time there is calm just knowing she is here.
We must face the challenges that everyone is facing;
Confront the fear that is mounting.
With my friend by my side I am a little less afraid.
Knowing I am not alone strengthens me; gives me hope.
We can face the world together.
We are not in this alone.
With my friend by my side, I rise up.
I am ready to be strong.

No Longer Lost in the Darkness

Life's journey continues with renewed hope.
A glimmer of light bursting through the darkness.
Days seem a bit brighter;
Nights, not quite so long.
A sense of strength envelops me.
I step forward;
Less timid, no longer afraid.
Each day brings new opportunities,
Chances to be whole.
I look at each day through a new lens;
See more clearly than I ever have before.
My journey has taken a novel turn.
It may not always be easy.
Twists and turns may lie ahead,
But now I know I can face them.
I am no longer lost in the darkness,
My path brightened by a light.

A Lighted Path

Shattered illusions once distracted me.
Now I cling to a new hope.
A light in the darkness beckons me,
Calls me forth and strengthens me.
I find hope in the future
As the pain of my present lessens.
My life spins in a new direction.
I travel a lighted path;
Step over stones that were once mountains.
Positive thoughts are no longer just an illusion.
My reality has shifted.
Hope has become my guiding light.
I breathe in fresh air and
Live with satisfaction as I begin anew.

A PHOENIX RISING

A poem seems a trite way to open this letter to you,
But it is all that I have.
All that I am.
You looked me in the eye and
Said you would be there.
I believed your lies;
Assumed you were telling me the truth.
Yet here I am without you;
Alone, as I always am.
No one lightens my load.
My hand is never held.
I suffer in silence,
Too embarrassed to call you out for abandoning me.
Day after day I continue
Living an existence where I alone feel the pain;
No one to dry my tears
Or tell me it will be okay.
You had the chance to save me;
An opportunity to make a difference.
Instead you left me here
To fend for myself and wither away,
But I am stronger than you think.
Like the phoenix, I will rise from the embers;
Find a way to make my life whole.
I will dry my eyes by the flame's blazing light.
My pains will ease,
Though they may always be a part of me.
I will move on.
Without you, stronger I will be!

A LIGHT EMERGES

Hope had faded.
I did not dare to believe that life would improve.
Living each day, merely going through the motions,
I had no reason to believe life would change.
Giving up seemed so much easier.
Still I found ways to continue.
Life dragged on day to day.
I became weary,
Tired and unwilling to try again.
The days were long.
The nights seemed endless.
I kept hearing there was a light out there somewhere,
But I could not find it.
Searching for a distant light seemed useless;
A waste of my time and the little energy I had left.
Then one day I was given a chance.
One that I had longed for, but did not believe existed.
That chance was a game changer.
My hope has been renewed.
What once seemed hopeless has materialized
And I have been given a new chance at life.

SO DEEP

Once again, I am falling into the pit of depression.
My will to participate in life dissipates.
I am left empty and lifeless as I stare at the walls that surround me.
In my mind I tell myself to stop tumbling;
Try to convince myself to take small steps toward interacting with others.
But these words fall upon deaf ears.
I am struggling just to make it through the day.
Curled up in a ball I lie in the darkness,
Afraid to allow myself to heal,
Unsure of how I fallen this low again.
I close my eyes;
Pretend I do not see just how much I am struggling.
Even though I know it is not true, I tell others I am okay.
I cannot continue like this.
The time has come to admit just how much help I really need.
I have fallen deeper than I thought;
Too deep to climb back up on my own.
I must reach out an unsteady hand;
Allow someone else to take hold.
I must admit I am in need of help;
Stop trying to survive on my own.
But what do I say?
How do I explain how lost I feel?
I am so far down I cannot see the surface.
Hope seems to be an effort in vain.
I need to reconnect my support system;
Allow myself to be helped.
Still I wonder if anyone can reach this low.
Am I savable?
I try to tell myself that I am.
If I reach up with the intent of making a conscious connection,
Someone will reach down for my hand.
This connection is all I can hope for;
All that I have left.

AVOIDANCE

I feel myself falling apart again.
Crumbling on the inside, I hide behind my façade;
Pretend that I am not worried;
Act as if it is all under control.
Inside is where the anxiety rips me; mocks me.
I attempt to be strong;
Try to act with my best interests as a priority,
But as so often happens, I fail.
I freeze, knowing what I have to do, but unable to take action.
I do not possess the strength I like to think I have.
Friends try to help, but I am weak.
I want to accept their assistance, but I shrivel into complacency.
With avoidance engrained within me,
I have learned to ignore problems until they hurt me;
Until problems anger me.
It is then that I am at a loss;
Unsure of how to continue and
Seeing avoidance as my only option.
I do not want my life to be this way,
But I struggle to find the inner strength to make changes.
I want to change.
I hear the rationale and understand that I cannot go on this way.
Yet I feel paralyzed.
The strength lies deep within me among the crumbled pieces of past failures.
I am left to question,
Am I ready to summon that strength to the surface?

WORDS

Can I listen without thinking?
Let the words fall where they may.
The words have their own purpose without me enforcing my perspective.
Sometimes words are just words, with no hidden meaning;
No secret agenda.
I must learn to listen with an open heart.
Keep my own words to myself until the time is right.
Words have power. Words hold truth.
But words also disguise lies.
I must allow myself to listen; to truly hear what is being spoken,
Withhold my judgment until the facts are known.
Listen not to reply, but to understand.

INVISIBLE WAR

An invisible battle against an illness others do not believe is real.
Despite wanting to give up,
I continue to fight.
I struggle to keep my life in balance,
Push the darkness behind me
And attempt to wear a smile.
I keep the pain hidden.
Tell others, "I am fine,"
When really I am barely holding my life together.
Hidden behind my white lies, depression pummels me;
Knocks me to the ground.
Still I climb back up;
Say that I am okay.
I cannot let the depression win,
Though I have grown tired of this endless battle.
Each day I drag out my battle gear, medication and therapy.
I continue on because I know no other way to live.
People look at me and do not see the daily battle I wage.
They do not see the pain in my eyes.
Like a soldier, I have learned to camouflage.
Others do not see the depression.
They do not know how hard I battle.
All they see is the mask I wear.
I cannot let them see the darkness that consumes me.
Others would not understand.
Sometimes I do not understand,
But I battle this invisible illness.
Determined to one day win the war.

STRONG WOMEN

Strong women—
Overcoming all that life has thrown at us.
Shared early memories shaped us;
Life separated us.
And then one day chance brought us back together.
Our struggles hidden for so long,
Believing we were alone.
We were trying to be so damn strong,
But our strength came from a bottle.
It numbed the world and allowed us to live a lie.
Until the day we found our own inner strength;
Took steps beyond our facades
And emerged anew.
No longer alone.
Drawn together by a common bond.
Led by a desire to be whole.
Strong women—
Who have overcome so much.

MY JOURNEY

I have learned to trust my journey.
It has been a hard and arduous journey,
But I have continued onward.
Long bouts of darkness have clouded my life;
Dragged me to depths I dare not describe.
Days seemed like nights;
My life blurring into one long day.
Specks of light have glimmered throughout my journey,
Many only pausing as they passed.
A few lights have guided my travels;
Remained by my side.
My journey has a purpose.
I travel through life for a reason.
Hope flickers in the distance.
Drawing me ever closer.
I know darkness will attempt to follow me;
Always be nearby,
But now I see a destination;
Grab onto the hope that beckons me.
I allow myself to continue on this journey
Though I take on a new role.
The journey no longer controls me.
I have become my own guide.
As I continue forth the light begins to shine more often,
Breaking through the dark clouds.
My journey will continue
As now I look forward with a smile,
Ready to embrace the light that guides me.

PILLARS OF STONE

Unaware of the transformation taking place within me,
I hide behind pillars of ice-cold stone.
This hiding place has become my home.
For so long I have been afraid to step outside its walls.
Here I know I am safe.
Inside of me, emotions are turning,
Attempting to catch my attention,
But I am so accustomed to being numb that I fail to notice.
Still something is changing,
Begging me to take notice.
Slowly I begin to become aware of the transformation.
I resist;
Cower behind my pillars,
But the transformation shakes me.
I begin to sweat as I wrap my arms around a pillar.
It crumples within my arms.
I am standing on my own,
No longer hidden.
A foreign feeling spreads through me.
It is strength,
A strength I did not know I possessed.
As the transformation continues, a smile forms on my face.
I am becoming someone new.
For the first time I realize I do not need to hide.
Stepping forward into the light, I allow myself to become whole.
No more hiding.
I have transformed into the woman I was meant to be.

THE MORNING LIGHT

Catch a glimpse of the morning light.
A new day has dawned,
Shining light on life;
Bringing hope to those who awaken their spirits.
Orange hues in the azure sky enliven nature.
Birds fly from their nests chirping sweet songs.
People emerge ready for the bustle of the new day.
The morning light holds hope;
Dreams ready to unfold.
The bright orange light climbs higher,
Warming the Earth,
Motivating people to live life to the fullest.
Each day is a unique gift,
A special chance to appreciate goodness
And hold dear all of life's splendor.

IN SEARCH OF A CRYSTAL BALL

Tommy sang about his search for a crystal ball.
I connected with his words;
Sought peace in his voice.
With my present marred by depression,
I long to know what the future holds.
I wonder if a crystal ball exists,
A glass orb to guide me.
Tommy, did you find your crystal ball?
Did it provide insight?
Or are you still alone?
Tell me, will I always be alone?
A crystal ball seems a simple concept.
Providing a chance to glimpse into the future;
An opportunity to see what it holds for me.
I will search for that crystal ball
And hope it brings me the answers that I seek.

WRITING TO HEAL

A Poem...

A poem is a small reminder of what my life has become.
The emotions, the thoughts form the lines.
Words bounce off the page;
Reflect the feelings I have held hidden for so long.

A poem holds my truth,
The essence of who I am.
Lines of verse provide insight;
Express the words I cannot speak.

A poem, all I have to offer.

WHERE ARE THE WORDS?

I am at a loss for words.
My pen has run dry.
The poetry that often flows has sputtered and come to a halt.
I search for the words;
Force ink upon the page,
But it makes no sense.
The words are just ramblings,
Meaningless and empty.
I can only wonder where their true meaning has gone.
This loss hurts;
Gnaws at my soul.
I can no longer explain my deepest feelings.
It as if I cannot speak.
The words must still be here.
But where are they hiding?
I search and search.
The words once comforted me; brought me peace.
Now they have escaped.
I must find them.
The words are my lifeline,
My reason for being.

THE WORDS FLED

My writing is stilted.
I write in pieces, unable to finish a poem.
Where has my muse hidden?
Where have the words fled to?
My hand shakes as I hold the pen.
Unsteady, leaving scratches on the page.
Poems left unfinished fill my journal,
As I wait for the words to flow once again.

THE WORDS PLAY GAMES

As I hold my pen over the page,
I wonder if the words will come.
They have been stubborn lately;
Only coming when they feel like it.
The words used to come whenever I needed them.
Ink flowed from my pen with ease,
But now I am left wondering where the words have gone.
I feel them inside of me
Even though they will not come out.
And then this happens.
I am stuck in the middle of a poem.
The words are playing their little game of hide and seek.
Trying to be patient, I look for the words;
Attempt to coax them out of their hiding spot.
"At least allow me to finish this poem," I call out.
A couple words peek out.
I grasp them;
Ink them on the page.
This poem will end here because
The other words are still hiding.

STILL I WRITE...

I express my fears through poetry;
Allow the written words to speak for me.
I am a poet, crafter of words,
But my words represent the brokenness that has consumed me.
The curative power of my writing has been lost.
As I write, the pain comes out, followed by fear.
This is anxiety.
Some say to take a deep breath and just relax.
It is not that easy.
Anxiety has a powerful grip like a chokehold.
The poetry I write gathers its strength from my anxiety.
That strength is fuel for the fire that builds with the intent to con-
sume me.
I question if I should continue to write;
Wonder if the words are hurting me.
Yet still my pen touches paper,
Scribbling the words that express my fear.

THE WORDS ARE STILL THERE

I try to calm myself.
Attempt to settle my fears.
I am weak.
I cannot do this alone,
But whom do I turn to in the middle of the night?
Everyone is asleep while I sit here writing.
My writing is an attempt to calm my thoughts.
I allow the words to pour from my pen, releasing painful emotions.
From time to time I glance up at the clock and
Wonder why the minutes tick so slowly.
I should be asleep, but anxiety allows sleep to elude me.
Words fill the page as each minute passes.
I have learned strategies to calm myself,
But none work once I have reached this point.
I can no longer breathe deeply.
It is too dark to go for a walk.
Self-hypnosis only works when I start it early enough.
I close my eyes and try to visualize that safe and serene place.
I know it is there, but I cannot reach it.
The anxiety pulsates through my body, leaving me shaking.
The poetry is supposed to be healing.
The words beating within my head are escaping onto the paper.
Unfortunately, new words quickly replace them.
I am not calm.
Calmness eludes me.
I lie here pen in hand, writing whatever comes out of my head,
But it does not make me feel any better.
I close my eyes, but the words are still there,
Screaming to escape onto the paper.

JUST WRITING

I am writing, but I feel lost;
Unsure of where the words will come from.
The flow of poetry has slowed;
Its rhythm lost.
Yet still my pen must scribble on the page.
The words inside of me find their way out.
Sometimes I do not understand them;
Wonder what they mean.
Other times I just write without thought.
Words emerge on the page;
Express the thoughts I was unaware of.
I am just writing,
Trying to let the words flow.
Building inside of me, the words need an outlet, a means to express
themselves.
As I write, I hope to find myself.

MY NEED

I need to write.
There is a longing within me,
But the words will not come.
My voice is trapped.
I try to force my pen but
The ink has run dry.
Where are the words that for so long flowed smoothly?
I feel the words inside of me attempting to make their escape.
I find a new pen.
The ink begins to spread on the page.
Words form lines.
Lines form a poem.
I am writing once again.

MERE SCRATCHES OF INK

Scratches of ink fill the page.
Forming words;
Transcribing thoughts.
An inner dialogue spilled onto the lines of my journal.
Words and more words.
My hand continues across the page.
I write to release the pain that fills my head.
Searching for clarity,
Attempting to make sense of the constant chatter.
I continue to write.
A poem takes shape.
The nonsense in my head makes sense on the page.
Poetry becomes an instrument of healing.
Each day I write,
Allowing the pain to be transformed.
Freeing my mind
Words carry meaning.
Poems speak to me
Mere scratches of ink;
A lifeline for my mind.

MY PEN

When my mind is full of turmoil, I turn to my pen,
Reach for my journal, and begin to write.
Words take the form of lines.
The poison pours out of me.
My pen is an instrument of healing.
The ink gives life to the words I cannot voice.
Line after line, page after page filled with my thoughts.
I feel each thought as it leaves my mind to make its mark upon the
paper.
The page soaks up my memories;
Becomes stained by my pain.
Dark thought after dark thought is released
And allowed to breathe on the page.
In these moments I feel lighter.
A sense of healing envelops me
As my turmoil escapes.
My pen provides this passage to healing.
Each poem I write gives me the courage to continue.
My journals hold the reality of my pain;
Relieving me of my pain
And allowing me to live.

THE PASSION IN MY VEINS

I need to write.
The passion flows through my veins.
As my pen glides across the page I feel most at ease.
Words emerge on the paper.
They were hidden inside of me, begging to escape.
My pen is my conduit.
The written word, a healing tool.
Gripping my pen, I let everything flow out of me.
Words emerge on the paper
They speak to me in a different voice.
Inside of me the words clamored, seemed senseless.
But on the lines of the paper I understand what they are expressing.
My thoughts make sense to me once they have been inked on the page.
I write because my life depends on it.
I need the words to make sense.
There is pain in these words.
There is passion.
The words are my deepest thoughts, my fears and anxieties.
Inside of me they hurt,
But on the page their power changes.
The words no longer cause pain.
They transform me; bring healing.
When ink spreads across the page, I feel myself healing.

The Gift of Poetry

Poetry is in my soul.
Not the "roses are red" lines,
But deep emotional words.
Gnawing at me;
Begging to be released through my pen.
So, I write.
Poems fill the pages of my journal.
The pain I have felt for so long emerges.

Poetry tells my story.
Relays the darkness that has consumed me.
The poetry forms deep within my darkness;
Flows out of me in a steady stream of words.
As I write, the pain eases.
I see a light that only the poetry carries.

Poetry is my healer.
The words enable me to understand my thoughts;
Allow me to emerge from the darkness
Into a world of light.
Poetry is my gift.

LAB COAT DIARIES

LIABILITY

WAITING

I am nervous.
The exam room makes me anxious.
My heartbeat races. My leg shakes.
Inside my head thoughts are whirling.
I stare at the linoleum floor.
It stares back at me.
Slowly the chest pain sneaks its way into my consciousness.
A chill runs through me.
Soon my anxiousness will freeze my words.
It always does.
I hate medical appointments.
Anxiety always overwhelms me;
Incapacitates me as I attempt to reach out for help.
The doctor enters the exam room.
I try to pretend that I am okay.
Looking down at the floor again, I avoid making eye contact.
The doctor does not notice.
Soon he will hand me a prescription and send me on my way.
The appointment will be over, but I will still feel anxious.

THE EXAM

I am anxious.
Or is paranoid a better description?
This happens every time,
But it seems to be getting worse.
The anxious thoughts fill my mind.
I see the exam room as it will be;
Feel as if I am already trapped within it.
I cannot control the thoughts.
The visions have a mind of their own.
So many previous attempts have ended in failure;
Left me to internalize ridicule.
Am I less of a woman because I am unable to get through this?
The doctor says to take Ativan as if that will solve the problem.
It won't. I have tried.
My mind is racing.
The anxiety has taken control.
The doctor will say reassuring words;
Try her best to keep me calm.
She will be confident that such a simple procedure can be done.
Until I let her down; let myself down.
I do not understand what happens.
My body closes up into some form of protection,
But I do not know what I am being protected from.
What happened to me?
The fear stems from something I have no conscious

awareness of;
No way to give words to my fears.
I wonder if I have suppressed something.
That seems to be the only explanation.
It is a simple exam.
Women go through it every day.
Why can't I?
There must be something wrong with me,
Something that has never healed.
I am unable to sleep knowing what tomorrow holds.
The doctor will try.
The Ativan will have the power of a piece of candy.
I will tense up.
The doctor will tell me to relax.
She will tell me I can do this,
But it will be too much for me.
Tears will fill my eyes.
Humiliation will take over my thoughts.
I will be a mess and the doctor will not have been able to
what she needed to do.
Embarrassed, I will not look up at her.
I will need more Ativan, but she will say I have had too
much already.
I am a failure as a woman,
Some type of damaged goods.
I am beyond repair.

MISDIAGNOSED

To the physician's assistant who labeled me catatonic,
I give you my sympathy.
You labeled me without understanding the diagnosis.
In your haste you used a term that does not describe me.
Look it up; read the diagnostic criteria.
Now look at me.
Really see me.
There is no catatonia, but that is the label you hung on me.
I do not meet the criteria for catatonia,
Not even close.

Yes, I suffer from depression.
That is part of my true diagnosis.
I have no problem admitting it.
If you are going to label my health condition, please do it correctly.
You would not mislabel a type of diabetes.
If I had cancer you would be sure to name the correct form.
Mental health disorders deserve the same consideration.

To the physician's assistant who gave me the wrong diagnosis,
I hand over my anger and frustration.
You did not take me seriously.
I hope that someday you will understand that mental health is a part
of total health.
You can never keep a person truly healthy,
If you do not respect that person's mental health as much as his or
her physical health.

To the physician's assistant who misdiagnosed me,
I offer my forgiveness in the hope that someday you will understand.

YOU COULD NOT BE BOTHERED

Dismissed as if my fears mean nothing.
You could not be bothered,
Could not spare even a few moments.
That is okay.
I actually understand.
It is not your fault.
You are the one who does not understand.
I asked you a simple question to ease my growing anxiety.
You gave me a two-letter response.
You did your job.
Why should it matter to you that your single word means nothing
to me?
It is as if you did not even answer,
But as I said, I understand.
You do not know what it is like to live with anxiety.
A few words from you might have calmed my fears,
Allowed me to stop thinking so much,
But you could not be bothered.
Now I know that I cannot expect anything from you.
I will not be so bold as to ask you a question again.
I mean nothing.
My worries are for me to deal with alone
Because you could not be bothered.

A Faceless Name on a Chart

I am just a faceless name on a chart;
A patient you need to push through as you move onto the next.
You pretend to listen, but you never really hear me.
Type something on a computer as if that will solve the problem.
Write a prescription for a medication that will not help me.
The pain I feel, the struggle I am faced with mean nothing to you.
I am just another chart to sign off on and forget.
Though you smile, you express no empathy.
I wonder if you really do not care or if you just do not understand.
Your words ring hollow.
You will not help me though you say you will.
Maybe I am to blame for believing you cared about your patients.
How many of us can you squeeze into your day?
It is all a numbers game.
As a patient, I do not matter.
I am not a person to you.
No longer will I waste your time.
My will to heal has been left shattered—
A victim of the care you failed to provide.

DO YOU REALLY SEE ME?

I get it.
I have a mental health disorder.
You do not understand.
I see you standing there in your white lab coat.
I guess you think I am crazy.
It is easier for you to just assume I am my mental illness.
You do not see the person behind the label.
The person who feels so deeply, who longs for life to be different.
That is who I really am.
I am not just "depressed with catatonic features."
I am more than my anxiety disorder.
I have dreams just like you.
I feel pain just like you.
Do you see me?
We are not that different.
One day you may struggle with this darkness, although I hope you do not.
I do not wish depression on anyone.
Sometimes I wish I could better explain what it feels like to live with a mental health disorder.
Let others know what it is like to see darkness all around.
I hide my tears, wear a fake smile just to get through the day.
You only see a part of me.
Deep inside I am longing to emerge from behind my diagnosis,
Shatter the label, and be seen.

BLIND TRUST

Blindly I trusted you.
Listened as you directed me.
Thought you were taking care of me,
But you just wrote prescription after prescription.
Told me to take this pill and that pill.
I did as you said;
Swallowed the pills,
But felt no relief.
The pills only masked my pain.
They did not heal me.
A fog descended upon me.
Your prescription pad caused it to thicken.
I did not know who I had become.
Barely recognized myself in the mirror.
I was going through the motions, not really living.
A deep darkness surrounded me.
Your answer was more pills.
A prescription pad always at the ready,
You passed me off with every signature.
I trusted you, but you offered no healing;
Provided no answers,
Only pills and more pills.
Until the pills became the sum of who I was.
For years I blindly listened to you;
Trusted you with my mental health,
But I was just a guinea pig to you.
I allowed you to experiment on me.
Medications you said were the answer drove me deeper

into the darkness;
Tore me down.
I faded faster with each pill I swallowed.
Until one day reality hit me in the face;
The realization that I should not have trusted you.
I should have asked questions,
Taken a role in my treatment.
So I walked away from you;
Sought help from others.
In time I stopped taking so many pills.
Found a psychiatrist who listens before she writes a pre-
scription;
Who does not solve everything with a pill;
Provides healing and an opportunity for me to live in a
world without the darkness.
No longer do I blindly trust.

An Illness

For many years I have fought an illness;
Battled it; been beaten by it.
This illness is invisible to those on the outside.
People who do not live with it cannot comprehend it.
They cannot fathom the pain it causes.
This pain cannot be measured with a doctor's instrument.
The symptoms are real;
Taking a toll on my desire to live.
The illness leaves me hopeless.
Doctors do not understand.
They merely slap a label on me and offer another useless prescription.
These doctors do not care if the label is correct.
The label does not have to provide a true picture of who I am or
What causes my suffering.
The prescriptions are bandages at best.
I have fought this illness for decades.
I know its ins and outs better than any medical professional,
But they do not listen to me;
Do not see me for who I am.
Doctors see the label and prescribe a pill.
That is not healthcare.
A true health professional would ask about my pain;
Would ask for my input and really listen to my answers.
A true healthcare professional would put me before the label
And seek to treat the whole of who I am.
I have a mental illness;
A type of illness that makes doctors uncomfortable.
They do not understand that mental health is a part of total health.
Until they reach this understanding, people with mental illness will
continue to suffer.

LIABILITY

Questioning my apprehension, I follow the nurse into the exam room.
Why do I still feel so anxious?
It has been almost three years.
I should be over it by now;
Forgotten those harsh words,
But I cannot let it go.
I am reminded at each medical visit.
Those words stung, pierced my very being.
The nurse tells me the PA will be right in to see me.
I nod and try to relax.
In a few moments a PA will enter the room.
The lab coat and stethoscope will be the same.
I remind myself that she is different.
She is not the PA who wounded me with her words,
But what if the lab coat and stethoscope are not the only similarities?
I know these thoughts are ridiculous,
But still my body starts to shake.
I will it to settle down.
There is a soft knock as the door opens.
The PA enters the exam room.
She smiles and asks how I am doing.
Inside, I feel myself fluttering.
I mumble that I am okay.
Trying to ease my anxiety, I focus on her questions.
The PA has no idea how anxious I am.
I could never bring myself to tell her.
This is not her fault.
While I have always been anxious,
One of her colleagues destroyed my trust;
Left me fearful that it will happen again.
Now I struggle to trust PAs and doctors.
All because of the insensitive words of one.

A Simple Question

You asked a question when I thought no one cared.
As you awaited my response, I saw the look in your eyes.
You really wanted to know my answer.
You cared when no one else did.
My reply was simple,
But you heard so much more.
The answer I gave was not enough.
You wanted to know more; to really understand.
So, you coaxed, and you prodded.
I did not know anything was wrong until you explained.
With heartfelt words and keen understanding, you took me in,
Enabled me to understand.
In that moment you changed my life.
You started my healing with one simple question;
Opened my eyes and
Gave me hope.
Today I reflect back on that moment.
I wonder if you know what a difference you made.
You stepped in when no one else could.
I am forever grateful that you took the time to ask a question
And listened for my answer.
You went beyond your role and made a difference.

A DOCTOR

Life is not simple when you struggle with depression and anxiety.
Simple acts seem monumental.
Medical appointments raise my anxiety level.
Going to the doctor is often preceded by a sleepless night.
When the doctor enters the exam room, my words become frozen.
I sound weak and frightened.
It takes a special doctor to walk in and understand.
A doctor who can separate the patient from the mental heath disorder
And hear the patient's true needs;
Listen and understand.
This doctor knows there is so much more to medicine than treating only what is seen.
This doctor sees the patient as a whole person;
As more than just a test result or surgical recovery.
This doctor truly listens and explains while comforting the patient.
This doctor guides the patient away from the anxiety.
This doctor truly understands that health is both physical and mental.
A doctor even the most anxious patient can trust.
A doctor truly worthy of her calling.

OUR SESSION

I walk into your office.
You greet me with a warm smile.
"How is it going?" you ask.
I shrug and tell you it is about the same.
You know there is more.
Instinctively, you begin to ask questions.
Assist me in discussing the depression that just will not go away.
It is at a level where I am functioning, but could easily fall down deeper.
You understand it better than I do.
We check in on the anxiety.
It has its moments.
We both know the recent triggers.
Discussing the triggers helps me make sense of them.
We talk about all that is going on without stopping to dwell too long.
When the time is right, you guide me through relaxation;
Suggest thoughts and ideas to help me move forward.
You bring me out of this hypnotic state,
Refreshed and ready to face the week.

A Lighthouse Standing Tall

For years you have guided me;
Held my emotions.
Lifted my mood and
Explained my pain.
You have allowed me to grow;
Enabled me to become myself.
Your words have counseled me.
You have made sense of my anxieties and
Eased my depression;
Given me a strength I did not know I possessed.
A voice of reason in my darkened world,
You have always known just what to say;
Understood how to bring me a bit of healing.
You have been there when there was no one else;
Provided comfort with your calm demeanor.
You are always there.
A lighthouse standing tall.
A beacon of light in the darkness.

HEARD

Calming words spoken with sincerity greet me.
A genuine interest in what I have to say,
Allowing me to feel at ease
And open up.
I have never trusted more than I do now.
No longer a mere bystander, I am a part of my healing.
My words are heard.
My thoughts are valued.
Questions intended to truly understand how I am doing guide our conversations.
Advice is given, but never preached.
It is safe to admit when I am not okay.
My thoughts are acknowledged;
My illness understood.
Guiding me on the road to healing,
A compassionate voice has restored my hope.

HEALING

Full of doubt and without hope, I entered;
Figuring I would go through another useless attempt to heal,
but not really believing.
I was met with positivity, friendly faces who did not push too hard.
Instead they welcomed me.
Explained what they were going to do;
Reassured me.

Transcranial magnetic stimulation, TMS, sounds like something out
of a sci-fi movie.
A machine seems a big leap from a bottle of pills and a stack of med-
icated patches.

Somehow the doctor persuaded me to give it a try.
The techs built trust with their caring words and gentle touch;
Always checking on me, making sure I was okay.

I sat there wondering what I was doing.
A magnetic device attached to my head.
Pulsating pokes somehow lifting the depression, taming the anxiety.
I wondered, *Could this device really work?*
Is it really making a difference?

After 30 years of struggling with depression, I never thought I could
find healing;
discover new hope in my life.
But TMS has given me just that.

Goodbye depression, once my sole companion.
Good riddance anxiety, once the tormentor of my mind and body.
Thank you TMS for giving me a new chance to truly experience life.

GRIEVING THROUGH POETRY

In Loving Memory of Daniel Capobianco

March 12, 1947 – September 13, 2009

CANCER RIPPED YOU AWAY

Cancer ripped you away too soon.
I watched you leave us as the disease attacked you with its full force.
You had so much life left to live,
So many memories left to create.
You were denied so much of life.
You cannot watch your grandchildren grow up,
Toss a baseball with your grandson,
Cheer for your granddaughter as she throws a runner out at second base.
You never walked me down the aisle.
No more trips to Hawaii with your wife
Or beers with your son.
Cancer ripped you away.
Your golden years were just beginning.
A lifetime of hard work and early mornings had earned you a retirement full of all you dreamed,
But your life was cut short.
You were taken from us, denied a part in our lives.
With tears in my eyes I wish we had had more time, made more memories.
I wish you were still with us,
But cancer ripped you away.

THE DREADED SENTENCE

So many people lost to a disease that knows no bounds;
A word no one wants to hear.
The diagnosis doctors despise making.
Cancer.
Cancer, the dreaded sentence,
Causing people to suffer as they battle for their lives.
No one is safe from its snare.
Babies, children, adults in the prime of their lives, the elderly—
All equal victims to this disease that cannot be denied.
Cancer.
Cancer, the dreaded sentence;
Attacking with an iron fist,
Tearing life from its victims.

CANCER

Cancer is an evil that must be destroyed.
It has taken too many lives.
I question the doctors who spend their lives researching a cure.
Why haven't they found one?
Is there some sort of conspiracy?
I cannot help but question.
Maybe I am speaking from a place of pain.
Maybe I am right.
There should be a cure by now.
Cancer has had its time.
But no cure will bring back those we have lost.

In Loving Memory of Burl H. Gray
March 12, 1915 – March 9, 2002

MEMORIES OF MY GRANDFATHER

An old Navy uniform hangs in my closet,
Untouched for decades.
A reminder of my grandfather,
A man of honor who served his country and loved his family.
He held my hand when I was a child,
Always had time for me.
When I would ask how he was doing,
I knew he would smile and reply,
"On top of the mountain."
Memories of him carrying buckets of water for his plants
Or taking something apart in his garage
Fill my heart.
Up at dawn, embracing life.
Ready to "see the country."
Nothing could slow him down.
Outfitted in simple work clothes;
Hands wrinkled and caked in dirt;
A bowl of ice cream each night while he watched the news;
Willing to help anyone in need.
He did everything his way,
The only way he knew how.
He lived to love my grandmother.
Treasured her, though he often drove her crazy.
Love was in their eyes.
My grandfather was a simple man;
A man of honor,
A man of love.
I hold onto my memories;
Cherish each moment I had with him
And hold him in my heart forever.

In Loving Memory of Katherine (Kay) Tropea Gray
October 27, 1917 – December 10, 2014

Whispers in the Night

Rosary beads in her hand
A recited prayer upon her lips
Dear ones held close at heart.

One bead after another she prayed
Soft whispers in the night
Calling on the Lord to bless her family and friends
Giving thanks for all she had.

Rosary beads in her hand night after night.
The Blessed Mother heard her petitions
And humbly brought them to the Lord.

One bead after another
She taught me to pray
Two whispers in the night.

AND MY HEART WAS
FILLED WITH LOVE

Today you would have been one hundred years old.
Though you are gone your love is still in my heart;
Still carries me through the difficult times.
I see you when I close my eyes;
See your smile and the joy on your face.
E li mio cuore é pieno d'amore.

You are standing in your kitchen,
Asking me questions, curious about my day.
Turning to your stove, you smile.
The aroma of onions and garlic, tomatoes and herbs, fill the kitchen.
E li mio cuore é pieno d'amore.

We continue talking, just you and me.
With a piece of bread, I taste your sauce.
You add another basil leaf.
I stir and watch the leaf disappear beneath the bubbling, red surface.
E li mio cuore é pieno d'amore.

So many memories flood my mind.
Your kitchen was a part of you.
We spent countless hours there.
A relationship beyond grandmother and granddaughter;
A true friendship, a special bond.
E li mio cuore é pieno d'amore.

I learned about love through your eyes.
You shared a special gift with me.
Love in the simple things—
Pasta boiling on the stove; cookies baking in the oven;
African violets on the window ledge; a smile upon a child's face.
E li mio cuore é pieno d'amore.

I wish I could turn back time and sit with you once more;
Tell you all that I feel, how much I miss you.
But time took you away, erased your hidden pain.
I know you are at peace.
E li mio cuore é pieno d'amore.

Even as I open my eyes, your love is in my heart forevermore.

In Loving Memory of Stella Capobianco
December 5, 1923 – March 31, 2017

MEMORIES OF STELLA

As a child I really did not know you.
I saw you two, maybe three times.
You moved to California when I was a teenager.
I did not know what to expect.
I wondered what you would be like.
Who was this woman I knew so little about?
I grew to love you even with your eccentricities.
Stella, a star, you always drew attention.
Stubborn and set in your ways,
But you let me in for a while.
Every year I took you to Midnight Mass on Christmas Eve;
Just you and me in the back row of the crowded church.
You told me stories of your younger days;
Laughed about all the pizza—though you pronounced it "beetza"—
you made for guests.
And how your house was always open.
You suffered the unbearable losses of your daughter, husband, and
son.
One day you could stand it no more and
Decided you would move back home to die.
I tried to convince you to stay with your grandchildren and
great-grandchildren in California,
But your mind was set.
You moved back to Pennsylvania to be near your husband's grave.
My only comfort was you had your dear sister-in-law by your side.
You lived much longer than you expected.
Then one day I received the call I did not want to receive.
You had passed away.
Reunited with lost loved ones,
Finally, at peace.

In Loving Memory of Carol A. Harrison
December 10, 1955 – May 17, 2018

MORE THAN YOU KNOW

A love of basketball brought us together.
Countless hours spent in the gym formed a bond between us.
Soon you would mean so much to me;
Influence me in so many ways.
You always knew just how far to push me;
The right words to say to inspire me.
That time could have ended when I graduated and moved away,
But you have always been there.
Always provided friendship and advice.
I have so many memories.
In a gym, you taught me how to teach.
In long-distance phone conversations and lengthy e-mails, you guided me.
Walking on the beach, picking up a sand dollar, you found a way to teach me about life and creating happiness.
I hear your voice advising without preaching when I need to make difficult decisions.
Your words pick me up; give me strength.
I am the woman I am today because you were always there.

TOO SOON

You left us too soon.
We still need you.
It is selfish of me to think this way,
But you have always been so important to me.
I cannot imagine not being able to turn to you for guidance.
Life is cruel;
Cancer even crueler.
It ripped you from us.
Forced you to suffer.
Brought you pain and affliction,
But you were strong.
Even when you knew the cancer would win,
You faced your battle with dignity,
A model for others throughout your suffering.
I will miss you;
Forever cherish your words of wisdom on the phone and
The long e-mails sharing your perspective.
How can you be gone?
It does not seem real.
My tears will continue to fall as I think about you.
My friend, my mentor, my coach, you will always be with me.

YOUR VOICE

I still hear your voice;
Genuineness in your words;
Always willing to talk when I needed someone.
You gave me a voice so many years ago.
I was quiet, but you heard something in me;
Found a way to guide the voice I had hidden for so long.
Through the years you have been there;
Witnessed my voice grow stronger.
A part of your voice is inside of me.
It can be heard when I reach out to others.
You are a piece of the teacher I have become.
I pass a part of you onto every student I teach, every girl I coach.
You are a part of the woman I am.
Your voice is in my heart,
Forever a piece of me.

CAROL'S GARDEN

Carol's Garden blossoms in her memory.
A shaman atop an old growth redwood stump extends his blessing and
    welcomes all to her garden.
Vibrant red rhododendrons bloom as the early spring brings sunshine to Fieldbrook.
Yellow tulips touch the garden with nature's gold.
Azaleas blossom into the bright colors Carol enjoyed, a reminder of her style.
Daffodils and Easter lilies fill the garden with more radiant colors.
A sturdy maple tree provides a canopy of protection.
Shades of green conifers soften the garden, a reminder of Carol's gentle heart.
Frogs and turtles made of stone dot the garden.
A butterfly in a heart invites loved ones to enjoy the garden.
Sitting quietly you can hear Carol's laughter in the breeze;
Feel her presence in the warm sunshine.
Loved ones and friends gather to share memories as they sit and cherish joyous times.
Carol's garden brings smiles to those who miss her.
Her smile fills the garden she so loved.
She is forever present in her garden.

FOREVER WITH YOU

With tears in your eyes you hold pain in your heart.
The loss you have suffered is immeasurable;
A vibrant life ripped away from you.
Your soul mate no longer stands beside you.
She resides in your heart.
Memories must sustain you now.
You have strength within you.
Love will carry you.
Your soul mate is with you always.
Present in your garden.
Smiling in the sunshine.
She is with you in the comfort of friends.
Dreams will bring her to you; hold you in the night.
Tears will dry as you remember the life you shared.
She is forever with you, always in your heart.

FLY

Many years ago, our lives' paths first crossed.
I was just starting out, a college freshman, lost and unsure of myself.
The day I walked into your office, my life changed forever,
Although it would take years for the changes to fully materialize.
The two of you welcomed me with smiles and wide-open arms.
I was timid, afraid of my own voice.
You both encouraged me, told me I would find my voice.
For several years I was underfoot; learning from you, picking up all I could.
You were my confidence when I could not find it on my own.
Building me up one step at a time.
Nudging me forward at times.
Giving me a firm push when I needed it.
Always smiling at my small achievements.
Gently pushing me away from the nest when my turn to fly arrived,
But always keeping a spot for me to fly home in times of need.
You gave me the wings to fly out on my own and
The strength and confidence to guide others.
Even as I began to do so, you were both always there for me.
Offering your wisdom and encouragement.
Still mentors and mentee, but even more so, friends now.
Every student, every athlete that I positively affect has been influenced by you.
Because without the two of you, I would be nothing.
Once many years ago you took in a timid 18-year-old,
Transformed me into the person you knew I could become.
Now almost 30 years later, I am the woman I was meant to be.
All because you embraced me and led the way.

CAROL'S PLACE

Many memories brought to mind today.
Smiles and laughter.
A team once connected gathered together many years later.
A time of happiness;
A moment to be honored,
But a piece of us is missing.
Leaving the moment bittersweet.

We know she is watching over us,
Present in our hearts.
As we enter into this great Hall, we know she is with us.
Smiling that smile of hers; laughing at memories.
Savoring every moment.
We each bring a piece of her with us.
Her encouragement set us each on our paths.
We remember her in our own ways.

The missing piece forever inside of us,
Entering this Hall with us.

In Memory of Marty Balin
January 30, 1942 – September 27, 2018
Singer – Jefferson Airplane

Sometimes the death of a celebrity or social figure touches us. I wrote this poem when Marty Balin of the Jefferson Airplane, a group that heavily influenced my teenage years, passed away.

A VOICE LOST

Another voice lost to us.
He will join heaven's rock band;
Sing with other legends;
A rich and tender voice lost to his earthly fans.
Greeted by his rock brethren, the stars lost before him.
Strumming a guitar, singing of miracles with a heavenly glow.
A voice of the "Summer of Love"
On a stage for decades,
Inspiring generations.
His earthly presence is gone,
But his voice lives on.

FOR DISCUSSION

One way to break down the stigma surrounding mental health is to have open discussions about it. I encourage you to read through these questions and answer them. Then engage in conversations with others.

General

1. Which poems resonate with/touch you? In what ways do the poems resonate?
2. What is your definition of darkness? How would you define light?
3. Light can be found amidst the darkness. In what ways does writing allow this to occur?
4. In what ways can dark poems be healing?
5. Read "An Invisible Illness" (page 58). How does finding out someone who appears to function well has a mental illness affect your impression of that person?

For Individuals Dealing with a Mental Health Disorder

1. Read the poem "My Journey" (page 49). Describe your healing journey. Where has it taken you? What ups and downs have you experienced on your journey?
2. How can you use writing to express the way mental illness affects you?
3. How can writing serve as healing tool for you?
4. Have you faced stigma because of your mental health disorder? If so, how has it impacted you?
5. Read "My Cracks" (page 57). How do your cracks strengthen you?
6. Read "Pillars of Stone" (page 75). What "pillars"

have you erected to protect you? How can you move beyond these "pillars"?

7. Read "My Need" (page 86). What "need" helps you cope with mental illness? What do you do when it is not working?

For the Loved Ones of Individuals with Mental Health Disorders

1. In what ways might reading a person's writing allow you to connect or relate to him or her better?
2. How can a person's writing inform the way you support this person?
3. What would you most like to say to your loved one with mental illness?
4. Read "A Friend" (page 64). How can you be a friend to someone with a mental health disorder?

For Healthcare Providers

1. How do you approach your patients with mental health disorders?
2. Have you ever made assumptions about a patient's mental health? What were those assumptions based on?
3. As a healthcare provider, how can you be more empathetic and understanding of your patients with mental health disorders?
4. Read the poem "Liability" (page 102). How might you recognize a patient's anxiety? How might you approach the patient?
5. Read "Misdiagnosed" (page 95). What is your level of understanding of mental health disorders? How comfortable are you with recognizing mental health disorders and treating patients with these disorders?
6. Read "A Simple Question" (page 103). How can you really listen to your patients?

For People Dealing with Grief

1. How can writing a poem help you through the grieving process?
2. How can writing keep memories of your loved ones alive?
3. Writing about a loved one forces you to focus your feelings. How can this allow you to grieve the person in a more personal way?
4. Think about a loved one who has passed away. What memories come to mind? How would you share those memories?

Paintings

To see the full color images, visit ginacapobianco.com or @shannon_feldmann_art on Instagram.

LIABILITY

CPSIA information can be obtained
at www.ICGtesting.com
Printed in the USA
LVHW020351091120
671124LV00017B/681